Lettuce

Mini
Growing
Guide

Edition 1

Lettuce Mini Growing Guide - Edition 1

By Lazaros' Blank Books
http://lazarosblankbooks.com
Text, Artwork & Design: Lazaros Georgoulas
lazageo@gmail.com

**Images by FreeImages.com/ Diego Medrano,
Rico Jensen, Ronaldo Taveira, veg92,
Dave Di Biase**

**Printed by CreateSpace, an Amazon.com
company.**

**ISBN-13: 978-1537410920
ISBN-10: 153741092X**

Lettuce,
Cool Season Vegetable

Lactuca Sativa
Asteraceae Family

What to know...

- Lettuce plants require full Sun for a good harvest. Shade is useful when the weather is hot.

- Lettuce is a cool season vegetable, adaptable to various growing conditions. Prefers temperatures around 60°F to 65°F (15°C to 18°C).

- Lettuce plants require a well-drained soil, well moisturized and with pH between 6.2 and 6.8.

- Lettuce has an annual lifecycle and is one of the easiest vegetables to grow.

- Lettuce plants reach from 0.5 to 2 ft. (15cm to 60cm) and spread from 0.5 to 1.5 ft. (15cm to 50cm).

- Lettuce's foliage color varies from light green, medium green and dark green to purple or red.

- Lettuce plants can handle light to moderate frost.

- Lettuce is not native to N.America and its origins come from the Mediterranean.

Lettuce Mini Growing Guide

Nice points... Can I have more growing details?

Sure here's what to do...

If you want to start by direct seed either indoors or in your garden, remember that germination temperatures are between 40°F and 85°F (5°C and 29°C).

Be careful of high temperatures or the seed will not germinate. Best germination temperature is 70°F (21°C). The baby Lettuce need 1-2 weeks to emerge.

You can have successful germination in 7 days at temperatures of 50°F (10°C). The Lettuce seed can be saved for more than a year in a cool and dry place.

Direct seed in your garden or transplant early in Spring. Be sure to work the soil well prior to planting. If you propagate by seed in your garden sow seeds 1/8" (or 0.3cm) deep, 1" (2.5cm) apart in rows 12" to 18" (30cm to 45cm) apart. You can later thin spacings when the young plants have 2 or more true leaves. If you start your seeds indoors then sow seeds in 1" (2.5cm) cups or cells about 4 weeks before transplanting in the garden. Do not plant seeds too deep as they need light to germinate.

Reduce water and temperature in order to harden plants prior to transplanting. Plants should be separated by 6" to 12" (15cm to 30cm) spacings in rows 18" (45cm) apart when planted in the garden.

Tip: In order to have a continuous Lettuce harvest you can plant several varieties with different maturity times. Also, schedule weekly or bi-weekly planting until the first frost comes.

How often do I need to water my Lettuce plants?

Lettuces have a shallow root system and they need constant moisture in order to flourish. Be sure to water your plants every day (preferably early in the morning). Most vegetables need daily watering so you can schedule a good time to supply your garden with water. Water your plants in the morning so they can survive the sunlight and heat of the day.`Water only when the soil is dry.

Tip: You can use row covers to protect your plants from pests and diseases. Use the covers before temperatures get too hot, then remove them.

What pests and diseases I should know about?

Control weeds in your garden and do not crowd plants to avoid most pests diseases. Also, do not forget to water when the soil dries.

Here are the most notable pests that could affect you Lettuce plants:
Aphids, Leafminers, Leafhoppers, Cabbage loopers, Cutworms, Wireworms and Slugs.

Diseases that could affect your plants are Damping Off, Downy Mildew, Mosaic and Fusarium

Four important factors to fight pests and avoid diseases:

[1] Pick strong, resistant varieties.

[2] Control weeds in your garden.

[3] Work the soil to improve air circulation.

[4] Avoid planting in the same space for 2-3 years.

Here ends the Lettuce Mini Growing Guide...

If you want to keep notes about your Lettuce growing progress you will find plenty of space in the following pages...

We wish you all the best.-

Lazaros' Blank Books

So you want to learn more
about Lazaros' Blank Books?
Visit...:

http://lazarosblankbooks.com

Made in the USA
Columbia, SC
11 July 2024

38492452R00033